PEVENSEY, WESTHAM
and District

A Portrait in Old Picture Postcards

by

David Brook

S.B. Publications

CONTENTS

HANKHAM & STONE CROSS

WESTHAM

PEVENSEY

PEVENSEY CASTLE

PEVENSEY VILLAGE

PEVENSEY PAGEANT

PEVENSEY BAY

NORMANS BAY

FOREWORD

I was particularly pleased when Westham historian David Brook invited me to write the foreword to this book.

In his book David has combined his extensive local knowledge together with photographs of postcards to produce a unique pictorial record of Pevensey, Westham and the surrounding areas.

It also gives me the opportunity to thank David for dedicating the proceeds from his book to the Carol Babb Cancer Trust. The trust has been set up in memory of Carol who was tragically afflicted with cancer and died in December 1991, aged 32.

Carol spent many of her childhood days with her sister Lynda at her grandparent's home in Hankham and also at their farm at Salt Marsh, Hailsham.

The aim of the Trust is to purchase a Magnetic Resonance Imaging (MRI) Scanner which will help in the earlier diagnosis and treatment of cancer.

Brian Babb
Trustee

INTRODUCTION

The picture postcards in this book, depicting the Parishes of Pevensey and Westham during the early years of this century, have been selected from David Brook's extensive collection.

You are taken on a leisurely walk through the hamlets of Hankham and Stone Cross into the villages of Westham and Pevensey, towards the coast at Pevensey Bay and finishing at Normans Bay.

It is interesting to note, that many of the same views today have hardly changed during the last eighty years. One can imagine the Edwardian photographer with his cumbersome tripod, brass-bound mahogany plate camera and accessories, wandering the quiet, relatively vehicle- free lanes and by-ways of the area, perhaps resting awhile at one of the many Tea Gardens, searching for his 'commercial' subjects.

The majority of the reproductions were postally used between 1906 to 1912, the classic 'Golden Age of Postcards', when the postage rate was only one half penny!!

John Vincent
Chairman
Pevensey and Westham Historical Society

vi

MAP OF THE AREA

This map, a copy of one produced by Christopher and John Greenwood in 1825, shows the route taken by the sequence of picture postcards. Starting in the north-west corner of the two parishes at 'Glenlye',through Hankham, Stone Cross, Westham, Pevensey, Pevensey Bay and finishing at the south east corner at Pevensey Sluice now called Normans Bay.

GREETINGS

AND · A · JOLLY · TIME · FULL · OF ·

PLEASANT · SURPRISES ·

from Hawkham

CHRISTMAS, 1917

This type of postcard was quite common up to the late 1930s for Christmas and birthdays. They were printed as a greetings card with the name of the town or village overprinted afterwards. This one was sent by two sisters to their parents at Peelings Farm.

GLENLEIGH MANOR, c. 1908

Originally built in the reign of Elizabeth I in 1508.In its time it has been a manor house, farm house, convent, hotel and now a religious centre. The original driveway came from the front door straight across the field to the lane from Hankham to the Hailsham Road. It was bought by Reginald Cunliffe Smith in 1904 and modernised, the outside being rendered. Before this it had been a building of red brick.The interior was completely destroyed by fire in the early 1970s and rebuilt, a new floor being added to the roof with additional bedrooms.

LUSTEDS, c. 1910

This was one of the oldest houses in Hankham until it was completely destroyed by fire in the mid 1930s. On the old Ordnance Survey map this house is shown as Horns, it stood on the south side of the road leading from Horns Corner on the Hankham to Glenleigh Road. A modern house with the same name now stands on the site although the old dairy and some old farm buildings still survive. The mis-spelling of Hankham was an error in spelling handed down in copying and not a 'Combe' as on the downs (from the Saxon).

HANKHAM STREET, c. 1910

This picture was taken from the north end of Hankham Street with the Dog House in the distance. The thatched flint buildings stood either side of the gateway to a large barn and cattle yard which were next to the house called Wychehurst. The barn was destroyed by fire in the 1950s.

HANKHAM TEA GARDENS, c. 1912

An early motor charabanc belonging to Chapmans of Eastbourne. They first came out from Eastbourne with horse-drawn buses to this popular venue. In the 1914-18 war, the charabancs had a hard roof fitted with a large bag filled with coal gas, strapped to the top due to the shortage of petrol. The tea gardens ceased to trade in the 1920s.

HANKHAM STREET, c. 1910

Hankham Street looking north and showing, on the right, the old blacksmith's shop which belonged to a Mr Ernest Thorpe. In 1886 it was listed as belonging to Thorpe, Mrs & Son, Hankham. He carried on the business until 1918 when it was bought by Mr W Reed, motor engineer, and it became a garage. All the buildings in the picture have now been demolished and replaced.

THE DOG HOUSE, c. 1908

This fine old house (c. 1600) was for many years divided up into three cottages. It was occupied by the army in the second world war and when returned for occupation afterwards was modernised and converted into one house. The tiles on the roof came from the Priory at Langney when it was demolished.

HANKHAM POST OFFICE, c. 1914

In the directory of 1870, Mr John Webber is listed as being postal receiver and shopkeeper at Hankham. By 1911 his daughter was running the business and continued to do so into the early 1940s, although the post office had been transferred to Mr Reed, motor engineer, in Hankham Street in 1939. The shop was situated in the end house of the Fostel buildings.

HANKHAM SCHOOL, c. 1905
The school opened on February 1st 1879 with 90 pupils; children walking to school from as far as Langney in the early days as this was then in Westham Parish. In recent years the school roll has fluctuated between 40 and 150 children.

CLASS PHOTOGHAPH, HANKHAM SCHOOL, c. 1904
The two teachers in this photograph were Mr C H Bennett, who was headmaster, and Miss Pilley who lived in Westham and married Mr Scotcher. The names of the children are not known, but it would be welcomed if some of the older inhabitants could put a name to some of the faces.

FOORDS LANE, c. 1912

This photograph, looking west, was taken from Hankham Hall Road with its junction with Foords Lane,shows the entrance to St Michael's House with a dog sitting at the gate. Next is Foords Cottage reputedly used by smugglers, with a stone chamber let into the kitchen floor now sealed off. The two pairs of weatherboard cottages were demolished in the 1960s to make way for modern bungalows.

ST MICHAEL AND ALL ANGELS, HANKHAM, 1917

Known locally as 'The Tin Church' because the roof was made of corrugated iron; the noise inside was quite deafening when there was a storm. The church ceased being a place of worship in 1928 when the new St. Luke's Church at Stone Cross was opened. The vicar was the Rev E. B. Davis who lived in St. Michael's House on the corner of Foords Lane and Hankham Hall Road. The church stood opposite the end of Foords Lane on the road from Stone Cross to Hankham at Hankham Cross.

PEELINGS, c. 1912

This is the oldest building in Hankham. The photograph shows two dormer windows in the roof. When extensive restoration work was carried out, and it was discovered to be of medieval origin, the dormer windows were removed and it is now restored to its original form.

STONE CROSS WAR MEMORIAL
An unusual view of Stone Cross War memorial as it was taken before St. Luke's Church was built. It now stands on the edge of the road but when it was first erected it was the same distance from the road as it is now from the church, the ground being taken for road widening. The poles in the background are hop poles as the land belonged to Peelings Manor where there are still oast houses to be seen.

STONE CROSS, c. 1908
Looking south from the Hailsham Road. The Red Lion Hotel is the main building, and the end wall and chimney on the extreme right of the picture is the old toll cottage on the turnpike road. The wall to the left of the sign post was part of the garden wall of the 'Walled-in House'. It enclosed an area from Stone Cross windmill down to the crossroads, south along the Eastbourne Road to the Walled-in House and then north east back up to the windmill; this last section still standing.

FLORAL RETREAT TEA GARDENS, c. 1908

This is the rear view of the tea gardens which stand at the crossroads at the north end of the High Street. The large Victorian building on the left is the Railway Hotel which was taken down in 1969 and replaced by houses. The Floral Retreat, now Swan Lake cafe, has not altered much in itself but the greenhouses and lawns have been covered by the garage next to the station and Montague Way estate. The lawn used to run down to a large lake, which was the old brickworks, and used for boating and fishing. The greenhouses were extensive and built all the way along the back of Gordon and Dansfield Terraces and then out to the railway line.

GONDOLA LAKE, c. 1900

This was a man-made lake excavated for the clay for the two brickworks which stood on the site; one being worked as early as 1851. All the bricks for the Victorian-type houses in Westham and Pevensey and also the bricks for the Grand Hotel in Eastbourne were made on this site. The ponds were filled in during the late 1960s and Montague Way estate next to the railway station was built. The further lakes were then filled in, and Church Bailey and the new doctor's surgery were built in the late 1980s.

WESTHAM HIGH STREET, c. 1910

Looking east along the High Street. The building on the far right, with the gas lamp in the front, was then called the Floral Retreat Tea Gardens. It had extensive greenhouses at the rear and the lake in the previous picture was used for fishing and boating. All the iron railings shown in the picture were dismantled and taken away to help with the war effort in the second world war.

STREET FARMHOUSE, c. 1908

There are three properties in the picture that are no longer standing. Street farmhouse on the extreme left, which stood on the corner of the High Street and Peelings Lane; it was demolished in the 1960s when the whole of the farm was sold for development and the road widened. The other properties are Myrtle Cottages, four very small low cottages that stood where Myrtle Court now stands next to the Pevensey Castle Hotel, and the coach house that stood between the cottages and the hotel.

THE HORSE POND, c. 1912

Looking east from Spring Cottages, the Horse Pond has changed a great deal in appearance. The road has been realigned and a brick wall and path with seats are in place in front of the grass verge. The wall behind has been replaced by bungalows, Downsview cottages had not been built, and the village hall now stands on the open ground next to the old blacksmith's and wheelwright's shop on the left.

WESTHAM POST OFFICE, c. 1910

Thornton and Sons occupied the Post office in the village baker's shop from 1907 until 1930 when the Post Office was transferred to the bakery owned by Mr Bowring at the corner of Peelings Lane and High Street. The shop front was enlarged when it was bought by Mr. Dallaway and opened as a butcher's shop. it was reinstated to its original design in the late 1980s. The old bakehouse stood at the rear of the building.

THE OLD HOUSES, c. 1916

The sign on the wall of the building on the right reads:-'T. R. Larkin, Harness Maker, Eastbourne and Hailsham, attends here every Tuesday.'Mr. Larkin used to travel round the local villages and there was a similar sign on the blacksmith's shop at Hankham but stating that Monday was his day of attendance. In older photographs, the Dial House, in the centre of the picture, is shown to have two doors opening onto the road; the other one being to the left of the man walking in the street. The large elm trees overhanging the footpath by the churchyard were taken down in the late 1970s.

THE DIAL HOUSE, c. 1906
One of the two oldest houses in the village. The door on the right has now been filled in, showing that it might have been two houses originally as it is now. At the turn of the century, the right-hand side ground floor was used as a boot and shoe repair shop worked by a Mr. Samuel Miller and Mr. Morley.

THE OAK HOUSE, c. 1906

This is probably the oldest house in the village, built in the late 1400s as a yeoman's house. As in the previous picture, the door on the right has now been blocked off. The house was the meeting place of Westham youth club before the second world war.

VIEW FROM CHURCH AVENUE, c. 1918
Church Avenue and the High Street were unmade roads at this time, with no pavements as we know them today. This view has not changed a great deal - except that the Oak House has now had the right-hand door blocked off and the chimney on the side of Church Farm House has been removed.

WESTHAM CHURCH, c. 1906

St. Mary's Church was built by the Normans in c. 1080. The original plan of the church was cruciform, consisting of a nave, chancel and north and south transepts; only the south wall, south transept and part of the north transept are the original Norman. Both the north and south transepts and the chancel probably had semi-circular apses on the east walls; the only signs of this now being some broken masonry outside the south transept. Extensive enlargements were carried out in the 14th century when the west tower was built.

27

WESTHAM CHURCH, c. 1904

This picture could no longer be taken today as the modern school building stands where the photographer was. The fence has been replaced with a stone wall and the two large trees have long gone. Note the three small Norman windows in the south wall with traces of a fourth window. To the left of the south door, there is a scratch dial which was used to tell the time of the services by placing a stick in the hole and seeing where the shadow fell. To the south of the small fir tree, in front of the south door, there are four stones about six inches square and nine inches high. these mark the site of the plague pit where people who died of the plague were buried.

INTERIOR OF WESTHAM CHURCH, c. 1908

The scene inside the church is much changed from when this picture was taken. The oil lamps have been replaced by electricity, the rood screen has been replaced after standing at the back of the church for many years, and in recent years the choir stalls have been moved into the body of the church in front of the rood screen. The screen was replaced as a memorial to members of the Welby family.

GENERAL VIEW, WESTHAM.

LOOKING WEST FROM THE CHURCH TOWER, c. 1918

The High Street can be seen in the foreground with the Pevensey Castle Hotel, to the rear of this view. On the far right can be seen the blacksmith's shop with the horse pond in front of it. The large building in the centre middle distance is the vicarage before the new bungalow was built in front. The houses on the far left are Park Villas, and the building in between was Vinall's, builder's workshop, now converted into a house. The access to the builder's yard and workshop was through the archway between numbers one and two Park Villas, next to the driveway to the vicarage. These properties are only visible in the photograph, as the properties in Pevensey Park Road had not been built at this time.

LOOKING EAST FROM THE CHURCH TOWER, c. 1906

Pevensey Church Tower can be seen behind the Norman castle with the roofs of The Gables house protruding above the Normal wall. In the centre, the Roman west gate can be seen with the outbuildings of Ivy Cottage against the wall. The large house is The Old Corner House before the two bay windows were added onto its frontage, and the roofs of Grace and Laurel cottages can also be seen. The house in the right foreground is the Old Vicarage.

WESTHAM STREET FROM THE EAST, c. 1910

In the distance can be seen Church Farm House with the Pevensey Castle Hozxtel behind; the flint wall on the right was removed when the road was altered in the 1960s. The wall on the extreme left was originally part of the old coalyard, the next two houses are Grace Cottage and Laurel Cottage with what was then a butcher's shop, later to become a grocers. Note the old gas lamp hanging outside the shop.

WESTHAM CHURCH FROM THE CASTLE, c. 1920
Looking through the Roman west gate towards Westham church with the roofs of the old vicarage in its foreground. The brick wall behind the gates has been replaced with a fence and the gates have been moved further into the castle so that the outlines of the Roman guardhouse could be outlined in stone.

Corporation Seal of Pevensey - Circa 1230 AD.

obverse

reverse

CORPORATION SEAL OF PEVENSEY, c.1230
This was the official seal of the Cinque Port of Pevensey which was a limb of the port of Hastings. It was engraved at the beginning of the thirteenth century and is still in the Courthouse Museum in the High Street. A translation of the inscriptions is as follows:- (obverse), The Seal of the Barons of Our Lord The King of England of Pevensey; (reverse), Saint Nicholas willingly guide and carry us to Pevensey.

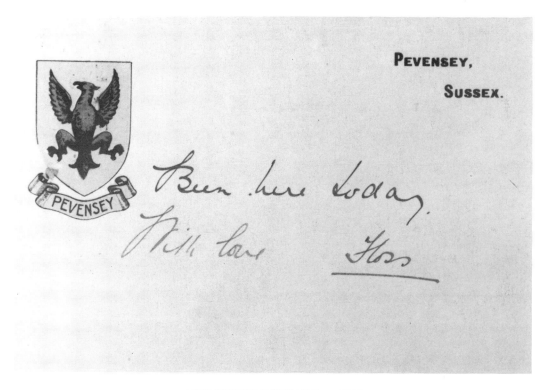

PEVENSEY,

SUSSEX.

Been here today.
With love
Flor

AN EARLY POSTCARD, c. 1900

From the look of the curt message on this card one would assume that the sender was not on very good terms with the recipient. The reason being, when postcards were first introduced and up to 1902 when the address side had the dividing line added down the centre, the message had to be printed on the other side and had to be less than five words otherwise it was classed as a letter and subject to the higher postage rate of one penny (1d).

IVY TEA GARDENS, c. 1910

At the eastern end of Westham Parish, the boundary with Pevensey runs along the centre of the road. This picture, although taken whilst standing in Westham, shows the Ivy Tea Gardens in Pevensey with its outbuildings built onto the west wall of the Roman castle. The road used to be the main A27 until the new road, to cut out the 90 degree corner, was built to the north of the Corner House from the church. The tea cottage was a favourite place for day trippers out from Eastbourne in the 1920s and 30s, but it was closed and demolished in the 1950s as it was condemned by the council as unfit.

CASTLE ROAD, c. 1920

The Gables is the house in the centre of the picture with Ivymead and Everstone on the left; the road had not been made up at this time. The bastion on the Roman wall of the castle had an extension built on top of it to form a watch tower probably in early Tudor times; the west wall only remaining in the picture. This was the view until the early 1940s when the hole was filled in and a small gun emplacement built behind it. The ivy on the walls was removed when the whole of the castle was renovated in the mid 1930s.

SUNDAY SCHOOL OUTING, 1906

Before the advent of mass transport, one of the highlights of the childrens' year was the Sunday school outing. Pevensey Castle was a very popular venue as can be seen from the picture and for some children it was the only time of the year they had an outing. After charabancs became more popular, they ventured farther afield and Bexhill seems to have been the favoured place for most of the schools from the Eastbourne, Hailsham, Lewes and Battle areas. The school party in the picture came from St. Andrew's School, Eastbourne which at that time would have been on the outskirts of the town.

THE ROMAN WEST GATE, c. 1910

These two bastions at the entrance to the Roman fortress formed the west gateway with the Roman road to the west leading through Polegate to Lewes. The guardroom was directly behind these gates. The two bastions. as with all the others along the Roman wall, were built on a formation of wooden beams resting on piles and infilled with chalk for the masonry walls to be built on top. The buildings abutting the castle wall were the outbuildings of the old Ivy Cottage Tea Rooms. Even at the time this picture was taken it was still a novelty to see a camera and people were anxious to have their photograph taken even if it was not for them.

PEVENSEY CASTLE, EASTBOURNE   37/70

THE NORMAN CASTLE, c. 1902
Taken from the south near the railway line and showing the commanding view the castle had over the
surrounding countryside, although when the Normans occupied the castle, the fields in the foreground
would have been tidal with some mud banks and channels leading to the sea. At this time the drawbridge
had not been replaced and the only access was from the east by the market.

HUNTING AT PEVENSEY, c. 1906

With the Pevensey Levels surrounding three sides of the castle, hunting has always been very popular because of the abundance of hares in the area; the hounds would have been from either Bexhill or Hailsham as these were the two main packs. The dress of the lady followers is very different from that which is worn today and would have certainly hindered them a great deal climbing over fences and styles.

Pevensey Castle

Dear Ethel, We enjoyed ourselves very much at Madam Susiaude's yesterday

A VICTORIAN POSTCARD, c. 1900
Although the view is very similar to the preceding pages, this card is included to show the artistic way in which some of the scenes were depicted. The ground surrounding the picture was a very pale green, with white water lilies with dark green leaves on the left and blue dragonflies at the top.

ENTRANCE TO INNER CASTLE, c. 1900

Although this is now the entrance to the inner castle, at the time of this photograph and until the mid 1930s when the castle was renovated, the entrance was round on the east side up the steps which are now the way out. There was no drawbridge and the arch at the gateway and the access to the dungeon were walled off. There was great excitement in the village when these two walls were removed, as well as all the masonry that had fallen down over the centuries from the two towers. Steps were found and subsequently excavated to reveal the castle's dungeon which was previously unknown. The two Edwardian ladies are seen picnicking beside the Elizabethan gun.

THE ELIZABETHAN GUN, c.1900

The gun has E R cast on its rear section which can be seen as a small upstand on the top, just in front of the rear brick support. It is a Demi-Culverin and has just over one foot of muzzle missing, probably blown off when firing. The round shot was four inches in diameter and weighed approximately eight pounds. The powder was a mixture of 25% each of sulphur and saltpetre, and 50% charcoal. The gun was removed in the late 1970s, mounted on a replica wooden gun carriage of the Elizabethan era and now stands by the west wall inside the Norman castle.

The Castle, Pevensey

THE NORMAN INTERIOR, c. 1920

The Eagle Tower had not been excavated at this time and it was possible to climb up to the height of the adjacent walls; the entrance as we know it today can be seen as the dark hole underneath the fallen rubble. Once this had all been removed, the oubliette in the base of the tower was revealed and the remains of the staircase to the upper rooms could be seen as well as the fireplace and chimney.

THE EAGLE TOWER GATEWAY, c. 1934

As can be seen from the previous picture the renovation was well under way by this time and the main gateway uncovered. The wall across the entrance leading to the steps to the dungeon had not been removed and it remained undiscovered. An Elizabethan fireplace was uncovered when the wall was removed, the catapult balls in front of the wall have now been cemented together in a pyramid as they were always being rolled into the dungeon by "passers - by".

THE NORMAN NORTH WALL, c. 1936

The north and east towers of the Norman castle had by this time had all the ivy removed from the walls and the moat had been cleared out. The small entrance to the left of the north tower had not had the grill fitted which is there today. Each of these towers consisted of three floors. The lower floor of the north tower, on the right, originally had a vaulted roof and was a chapel; the remains of the vaulting can still be seen on the sides of the walls.

PEVENSEY FROM THE CASTLE, c. 1900

The Royal Oak is on the left of the picture, with the four cottages belonging to it at the rear facing Pevensey Street. The porch at the front of the hotel and also the small gardens each side are on land owned by the Town Trust, with a rental of sixpence a year payable. The white glazed building in the right foreground stood in the market grounds and had the weighbridge outside with the scales and recorder inside, it was also used as the market office. At this time the churchyard had not been extended and was still an orchard belonging to the farm.

Peeps from Pevensey Castle No 2, showing Pevensey Village.

PEVENSEY FROM THE EAST CASTLE GATE, c. 1904

By the height of the gate from the road one can see that there has been much alteration work done on the gateway. There were ten steps up into the castle from the road where the slope now is. The double brick arch was removed in 1936 along with these steps and the gate positioned some twenty-five feet inside the castle with a surrounding fence to keep in livestock.

49

PEVENSEY FROM THE AIR, c. 1933

The new road in the top left-hand corner had just been finished but it is not the long awaited bypass but the new road to Bexhill, the old one is visible to the right. There are only six houses from Fence bridge to the level crossing but the Street itself has not changed much apart from the rebuilding of the council houses in the late 1980s. The Roman fortress which enclosed about eleven acres dominates the picture, with the smaller Norman castle in the south-eastern corner. At the bottom of the picture adjoining the north-west bastion of the Roman wall, the remains of the old village Pound for keeping stray animals can be seen and the roofs of Ivy Cottage to the right towards the west gate.

ROMAN EAST GATE, c. 1908

As can be seen in the photograph, the castle was a popular place for many people who had taken up cycling, although some of them still preferred to travel in the comfort of a horse and carriage evidenced by the lady and gentleman at the bottom of the steps. The gardens of the Castle Tea gardens had yet to be laid out, with the rose arches over the path as so many residents remember them; the area still used as a farmyard. Notice the haystack behind the coachman on the carriage.

THE MINT HOUSE PEVENSEY

THE MINT HOUSE, c. 1900

Taken from on top of the castle wall behind the tea rooms, the Mint House retains a similar exterior appearance today. At the time of this photograph, the building was occupied by three cottages; the middle one being the village shop. The greenhouses at the rear belonged to Harold Lodge, now Priory Court Hotel, which was run as a florist and nursery. The Mint House acquired the land and built workshops on it when it was opened as an antique shop owned by Charles Allen in the early 1900s. The building itself was built on the site of the old Pevensey mint.

Mint House — Pevensey.

PEVENSEY STREET, c. 1912

The pace of life was somewhat slower in this photograph than it is today. The Mint House on the left has changed considerably in appearance from the previous postcard; now having the imposing title of "The Historical Old Mint House" and converted from the three original cottages into one of the largest antique shops in the south of England at that time. It was well advertised and had a very large advertising board on the local station. The old Farmhouse can be seen further down the street with the old Courthouse opposite.

THE MARKET SQUARE, c. 1920

The market square between the castle walls and the Royal Oak Hotel is now used solely as a car park. It was probably a Tuesday, on market day, when this picture was taken. The drover, on the left nearest the castle, was Mr Ernie Funnell. The other man is unknown.

ST. NICHOLAS' CHURCH FROM THE MARSH, c. 1920

From what is now an extension of the recreation ground, the wall of the market can be seen with the rails of the cattle stalls projecting above it. The small building on the left housed the cowstalls belonging to Mr Covell of Church Farm. Mr Covell had the milk round in both the villages of Pevensey and Westham; he ceased trading in the 1960s and his milk round was taken over by Mr E Banks of Bridge Farm. The church of St. Nicholas is in the background with the vicarage hidden behind the fir trees.

Entrance to Pevensey Castle from Miss Covells.

ENTRANCE TO PEVENSEY CASTLE, c. 1900

The caption on this postcard would be somewhat mystifying to anyone visiting the castle today. The reason being that until the drawbridge was replaced, the only way into the castle was up the steps by the side of the tea rooms in the centre of the picture. The wall the gentleman is sitting on is now part of the churchyard but was then a garden and an orchard belonging to the tea rooms. The tea rooms were run by a Mr Covell who was also custodian of the castle, and they remained in the family until it closed in the 1960s. It has now been bought by English Heritage and leased out; the rear room being the tourist office and the rest of the building a well equipped and pleasant restaurant.

PEVENSEY CHURCH, c. 1900

The church, dedicated to St. Nicholas, dates from the early 13th century and is built of green sandstone probably from the quarry that existed in Eastbourne in earlier times. The spire to the church, before its restoration, began at the line of bricks below the wooden louvres in the picture, with a chimney protruding from the north-east corner. At the opening of the church, after restoration in 1877, the Corporation attended in state accompanied by the mace-bearer. The clock on the east and west faces of the tower was installed in 1908.

THE CHURCH INTERIOR, c. 1910

The chancel of the church in relation to the nave is very long compared with many other churches. One unusual feature of the church is the alternating pillars of octagonal and clustered construction. Note the oil lamps hanging from the roof which were the only form of lighting until electricity was installed.In the late 1600s the chancel was completely cut off from the nave by a wall across the chancel arch. The chancel fell into disrepair and one of the local inhabitants' ancestors kept cattle inside. It was also used as a store for coal for a time and a hiding place for contraband by local smugglers.

THE OLD COURTHOUSE, c. 1908

The interior of the Old Courthouse is still as it was when it was used by the judiciary in earlier days. It has a small dock for the accused to stand in, a bench for the magistrate and seats at the side for the jury. Below the court, there are two cells and a small exercise yard. In the second world war the cells were used as a local mortuary. The Courthouse is now used as a local museum housing much of the history of Pevensey including the corporation seal, the official weights and measures and many fascinating exhibits.

PEVENSEY STREET, c. 1906

Looking east along Pevensey Street, the Old Courthouse is on the right with the Old Farmhouse opposite; this house has been extended to take in the yard on the left so that the external chimney now protrudes through the roof altering the appearance considerably. The old farm buildings can be seen on the right behind the high wall; this area is now the village allotments. The next building with the Georgian facade is the Smugglers Inn known previously as the New Inn.

THE NEW INN, c. 1910

Now called The Smugglers, the Georgian front of the New Inn has now been extended to the end of the building to cover the sloping roof, and the gateway and low wall leading to the stables have been removed. The sign on the gable end of the inn reads: Southdown and East Grinstead Breweries Ltd, Ales & Stouts.

PEVENSEY FIRE ENGINE, c. 1911

Photographed outside the old Eastbourne Fire Station in the old Institute building in Grove Road, this hand-operated, horse-drawn appliance had just been painted in its new livery and was awaiting delivery to Pevensey after its acquisition secondhand from Eastbourne Fire Brigade. The pump was bought and presented to the village by Mr Charles Allen, owner of the Mint House.

LOOKING WEST TO THE CASTLE, c. 1910

The wall on the right and the orchard and garden to the New Inn have given way to the pressures of modern life and become a car park. This view of the inn has not changed, but the small square building opposite, that housed the Post Office, has been removed from the front of the house.

THE OLD SHOP, c. 1908

The sign on the side of the wall reads: G Watson, dairyman and carman, the building being the cart lodge to the farmhouse adjoining which was his residence. The rather untidy gathering of sheds next door was the village shop which is now the Post Office and stores. Camden Cottage is next and the end of the terrace of Kings Cottages can be seen at the far end of the street.

THE OLD THATCH, c. 1900
This charming old world cottage used to stand halfway between the entrance to the recreation ground and Church Lane in Wallsend Road. A more elaborate thatch was built on the sight during the mid 1930s.

THE THATCHED HOUSE PEVENSEY, c. 1938

This rather grand building in the village replaced the one in the previous picture. It was opened as a "Road and Guest House", with music provided for dancing during the afternoon and evening. All guests were invited to become members of the Social Club. Thine Host, as the advertisements said, was a Mr Li Chun Pay. Was this the first Chinese restaurant in Sussex? During the second world war, the building was occupied by the Army and used as an officer's mess. Tragically, it was destroyed by fire in May 1944.

VIEW FROM RIVER HAVEN, c. 1910

With the building of the Pevensey bypass, the scene from Broadwater, as it was known to the local residents, on the Wartling Road has changed out of all recognition. A new cut has been excavated where the river bends and the horseshoe bend is no longer there; this part of the river has been filled in and a new bridge built. The old houses consisting of King's Cottages, Camden Cottage, Penthouse Cottages and the New Inn are on the left, with the church and vicarage behind the trees, and the walls of the castle standing up behind the houses at the west end of the village on the right.

FENCE BRIDGE, PEVENSEY, c. 1906

The road from Pevensey Bay station to Pevensey at Fence Bridge looking north west. The castle and church can be seen in the background and the thatched roof of the cottage in the previous picture can be seen behind the bungalow. The building in the centre foreground was built as refreshment rooms at the turn of the century The new course for the river, as it is today, was cut through in the autumn of 1979, as the road from Fence Bridge down as far as the level crossing was subsiding into the river due to the heavy traffic that now uses the road.

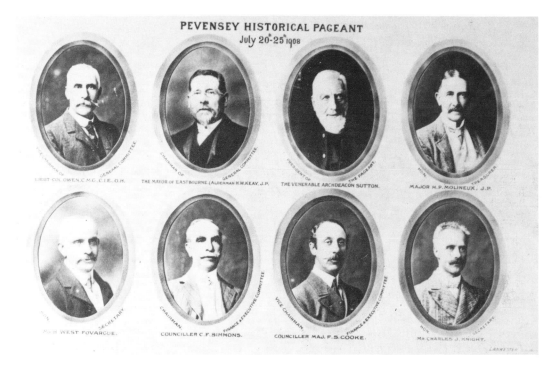

PEVENSEY HISTORICAL PAGEANT
July 20-25 1908

LIEUT-COL OWEN, C.M.G., C.I.E., O.H.

THE MAYOR OF EASTBOURNE (ALDERMAN H.W.KEAY, J.P.

THE VENERABLE ARCHDEACON SUTTON.

MAJOR H.P. MOLINEUX, J.P.

WEST FOVARGUE.

COUNCILLER C.F. SIMMONS.

COUNCILLER MAJ. F.S. COOKE.

Mr CHARLES J. KNIGHT.

PEVENSEY PAGEANT, c. 1908

This was the biggest event to be held in Pevensey for centuries. The organisation of the Pageant was tremendous as each town and village that took part did their own scene. It started with a service in the church and then a procession to the castle for the last hymeThis picture shows just eight of those who were on the committee, others having such grand titles as Master of the Music, Master of the Horse, Mistress of the Robes and author of the Book of Words.

69

THE PAGEANT: THE COMING OF CHRISTIANITY
This episode of the pageant was performed by residents of Bexhill. Whoever sent the original postcard must have known some of the people taking part as one or two of the actors have had numbers written on them. A typical photograph showing the effort that went into the making of the costumes and accessories from all the local villages and towns.

THE PAGEANT: BISHOP ODO BESIEGED

As can be seen from the postcard the costumes for the pageant were very elaborate; the only exception is the gentleman on the right being carried on the bier by two soldiers. Closer examination shows he is wearing a suit, collar and tie and has a cloth cap on his head. It is possible that the photographer commissioned for the pageant wanted to be in one of the hundred and more postcards that were on sale for the event.

PEVENSEY HISTORICAL PAGEANT. Episode IX. A Tale of the Smuggling Days. A.D. 1746.   COPYRIGHT LANKESTER, TUN. WE

THE PAGEANT: A TALE OF SMUGGLING DAYS

In the past, one of the more common and profitable pastimes of the community from the surrounding district was smuggling, as depicted in this scene showing a band of smugglers being caught by the revenue men, forerunners of our Customs Officers. A local curate, Mr W Leeke, recalls in 1841 how, when returning from Hankham one dark night with his wife, they hid in the hedge as a body of men, about seventy strong, passed by silently who were obviously smugglers returning from Pevensey Bay on their way to Hailsham.

THE PAGEANT: ANDREW BORDE AND FOLLOWERS

As well as all the postcards of the main tableaux in the pageant, there were many produced giving close ups of individuals and groups. Each event was depicted by a local village or town and this photograph shows the group from Pevensey and Westham. The man on the right of Andrew Borde has been identified as Mr Frederick Tapp who lived in Rattle Road, Westham.

THE POST OFFICE, PEVENSEY BAY, c. 1906

Known by older inhabitants as Holman's Corner, Castle View House stands at the crossroads at the end of the road from Pevensey. It was owned by a Mrs Sara Beal and run as a dairy and Post Office until about 1919, when it was taken over by a relative until 1924. When the dairy was transferred to North Road, the Post Office was taken over by F. C Botwright and sons and combined as a general stores. Later on it became Holmans Stores. The downstairs front room of the weatherboarded house next to it was later turned into a shop. Standing on the skyline is Red House with a small wooden building at the side used as a cafe; the buildings were destroyed by a bomb in the second world war. It is hard to imagine anybody being able to stand in the middle of the crossroads and hold a conversation today!

THE BEACH TOWARDS LANGNEY POINT, c. 1902
A fine view of Pevensey Bay photographed before the groynes were put in place to stop the beach being washed away. Tower 61 is behind the houses on the right and the boy is sitting adjacent to the end of Collier Road.

TOWER 61, c. 1910

One of the many Martello Towers built between 1804 and 1809 along the south coast as part of the coasted defences against the serious threat of invasion by France. With walls seven to eight foot thick, they had a single traversing gun on the roof and were manned by soldiers in rotation who were based at the barracks south of Peelings Lane, Westham, now Castle View Gardens. The houses on the right are in Western Road and the small white building on the left is the Castle Hotel along with other houses in Eastbourne Road. The beach area in the foreground is now part of the Rosetti Road estate.

VIEW FROM TOWER 61

Photographed from the top of the tower, which was converted into a house in the late 1980s, the Castle Hotel can be seen on the left with North Terrace behind. The low roofs of the Cabins, which were built in 1847, are in the middle of the picture. On the road behind, that goes to Pevensey, are a line of four horse and carts probably carrying either beach for building or coal. The coal ships used to unload at the end of Collier Road and the coal was taken to one of the coalyards in Pevensey Bay by horse and cart. On the far right can be seen Richmond House with the top of the Bay Hotel in the distance. It has not yet been possible to identify the square building in the centre and any information would be welcome.

RICHMOND HOUSE, c. 1910

Only Richmond House (a boarding house) and the Bay Hotel stood on this part of the High Street up to Collier Road at this time. Note the construction of the open window on the first floor with the square pane and the rounded moulding at the top to fit into the rounded arch of the brickwork. A parade of shops with flats above were built on the open ground to the right in the 1960s.

Bay Hotel, Pevensey.

THE BAY HOTEL, c. 1910

The Bay Hotel was built in the late 1880s; the wooden verandah and the pillared wall have now been replaced by a brick construction and where the fence stands the bakery and cafe now stand. A block of flats was built on the open space in front of the hotel in the late 1980s.

ST. WILFRED'S CHURCH AND BAY HOTEL, c. 1906

Looking west from what is now Marine Road, there are no buildings in either Collier or Bay Roads. The Honeypot tea rooms were built later on the open space in the foreground. The Bay Hotel and Richmond House are on the right, with the free church after the gap. On the left of the road is St. Wilfred's Church which was built in 1881 and demolished in 1971 when a row of shops and flats were built.

THE LIDO, c. 1930

This 1930s cafe used to supply teas and ice creams to the holidaymakers who came to Pevensey Bay and also the day trippers who came out from Eastbourne. The Red House is on the left and the small cubicles on the right were changing huts for bathers. It was demolished after the war and the Nevada cafe built in it place.

PEVENSEY BAY AND SOUTH DOWNS.   6783

AERIAL VIEW OF PEVENSEY BAY, c. 1946

Tower 61 can be seen behind the houses on the left, and the car park, with cars up to the edge of the beach, to the left of the Lido. To the left of the open space behind is Collier Road, with some of the wartime tank traps laying in the hollow to the east, and St Wilfred's Church at the rear.

BEACHLANDS ESTATE, c. 1938

Beachlands Estate starts where Red House farm used to stand on the north side of the coast road. Keith Martin the builder started erecting these bungalows in 1934; the original prices starting at £495.00. Note the vast stretch of shingle bank that then existed between the garden fences of the bungalows and high-water mark. The high-tide mark is now only about eight to ten feet from the fences in places and the sea reaches the bungalows in very rough weather. In the second world war, this whole stretch of coastline through to Eastbourne had two rows of concrete tank traps, scaffolding at the top of the beach and fifteen-foot-high scaffolding on the sands as protection against the threat of invasion.

MARTELLO TOWER, NORMANS BAY

TOWER 55, NORMAN'S BAY

This is the only Martello tower remaining between Cooden and tower 61 at Pevensey Bay. Four towers have been washed into the sea between tower 61 and Cooden, and there was also a tower near where the Cooden Beach Hotel now stands. These towers were erected from 1805 onwards as the threat from Napoleon became serious; luckily they never had to be used. They were then taken over by the excise men in their fight against smuggling. The tower was taken over by the military in the second world war after it had been used as a private residence for many years.

NORMANS BAY HALT, c. 1933

Until its opening in 1905, the hamlet had been known only as Pevensey Sluice; its name coming from the sluice gates on the river. The halt at this time had only a wooden platform and the ticket office had not yet been built. The line was electrified in 1935 when the third rail was added. The gate keeper's cottage on the down side in the picture has now been demolished and the row of six coastguard cottages have had houses built all around them.

NORMANS BAY CHURCH, c. 1914

The church was built on land given by the Duke of Devonshire in 1866. Canon Simpson had it erected partly because of the number of families attached to the coastguard station. The Church was dedicated to St. James after the chapel of St James that was situated in the ancient village of Northeye, now lost, to the north-east of the Star Inn. Under a special dispensation, it also served as the village school with three classrooms and seating for thirty-five pupils. The building was demolished in the mid 1970s and two modern houses erected on the site.

ALICE'S SHOP, c. 1940

Had the writer of the caption "Shopping Centre" looked into a crystal ball and foreseen the potential of the now familiar out-of-town shopping centres? Sadly this shop could not stand the competition and has now closed. Alice's will be remembered with affection by the many holidaymakers who shopped there as well as the local residents who patronised her during the lean winter months.

THE STAR INN, c. 1935
Built as a sluice-keepers' cottage at the beginning of the fifteenth century, when the draining of the marshes was of the utmost importance for the rearing of sheep and cattle. By the end of the sixteenth century it was no longer needed for the purpose and sold to become an inn. The Star of Bethlehem, as it was first known, later to be called The Star, has had a long connection with smuggling over the centuries. It is no longer the little pub on the marsh but has been modernised and a large restaurant added on its west side.

PEVENSEY SLUICE SIGNAL-BOX, c. 1915

This signal-box stood at the far end of what is now Normans Bay, where the road crosses the railway line at the eastern end of Cooden golf course. It was built during the first world war when the military were encamped on the golf course, controlling the siding off the main line into the camp for the unloading of provisions and stores.

PEVENSEY SLUICE

NORMANS BAY SLUICE, c. 1916

Pevensey Sluice, the original name for the hamlet, derived from the time Pevensey Levels were drained, with the sluice providing the main river outlet to the sea. The main problem was how to stop the surge of sea water onto the levels at high tide. This was overcame by building hutches (ducts) through the beach bank, with backflow gates at the seaward end which closed automatically when the tidal pressure was greater than the freshwater outflow. To reduce the pressure in the duct from the build up of water from the levels at high tide, boilers (brick or metal vents) were built into the top of the hutches - as can be seen above over the top of the archway with the backflow gates below.